MW00450385

What Everyone Should Know About
NIGERIAN HISTORY, POLITICS
& GOVERNMENT

By Victor Anazonwu

© 2017

All rights reserved. Except for quotations, no part of
this book may be reproduced without prior written
permission from the publisher.

ISBN 9781973253488

Published by Elipses Ltd., Plot 4, Block B8,
CMD/Jubilee Road, Magodo GRA, Lagos, Nigeria
Tel: +234 7033271909

Dedication

This book is dedicated
to the memory of Professor Adiele Afigbo.
He was my history teacher and mentor.

Acknowledgements

Inspiration for this book came from a discussion with my teenage son. He had chosen to study one of the business disciplines at university and wondered why he was still expected to take courses in Politics, Government, History and Philosophy. In the course of explaining this to him, I realized that he considered those subjects burdensome, long and windy. I observed that the problem was more with presentation than substance. I decided to be part of the solution to this problem by offering a simplified and unified volume covering only the most essential topics for everyone - whatever their discipline. Thanks, Ralu, for opening my eyes.

To Mr. Isaac Acho, veteran book editor and good friend, I owe a debt of gratitude for guidance on the structure of this book. He patiently read my first drat manuscript and made vital suggestions for better configuring the content and audience. I was encouraged by his feedback.

To my wife, Ngozi, I say thank you for patiently bearing with me all those days and nights when I spent countless hours scribbling my notes, researching the subjects or typing my manuscripts. Finally I am grateful to God for endless graces. He makes all good things possible.

Introduction

This book is conceived as a quick and handy reference for all, especially students interested in grasping the roots and essence of Nigeria's governmental and political history with minimum hassle. Those who wish may then go into detailed study of specific topics and periods for further enlightenment.

It highlights some of the political systems prevalent in the territory before and at the time of arrival of British explorers, missionaries and colonizers. It chronicles the roles played by British colonial officials in forming the country and shaping its fortunes. It discusses the major personalities, events, constitutional systems, principles and motives at work throughout the period covered. It analyses the rise of nationalist sentiments and the slow, difficult journey to independence. It summarizes the events leading to the demise of the First Republic, the onset of military governments and the outbreak of civil war. It provides a simple framework for understanding the development of modern political parties in the country since the first one appeared in 1923.

The style of presentation is deliberately brief, simple and easy to read. Pictures and illustrations are used to enliven the reading experience. This is informed by the understanding that the account of our collective past is best presented in ways easily accessible to all. The more people know about their past, the better their chances of avoiding old mistakes, and succeeding today and in the future.

Table of Contents

Chapter 1: Pre-Colonial Systems of Government

In the century before colonial rule started in what later came to be called Nigeria, there were many systems of government among the different peoples and communities. They varied from placed to place and from one culture to another. In broad outline, they included the larger political units of Sokoto Caliphate and Bornu in the North; the medium-sized governmental systems of Oyo, Nupe and Benin in the South-West and Middle Belt; and the smaller city-state and republican systems of the South-East and South-South.

Three of them are discussed here:
• The Caliphate System in Northern Nigeria
• The Empire System in Oyo, Western Nigeria
• And the Republican System among the Igbos of South-East Nigeria.

Over the period 1849 to 1903, these different peoples, cultures and political systems were gradually brought under British influence by force, threat of force and dubious treaties. This was done by agents of the Royal Niger Company, acting on behalf of the British crown.

It was made possible by two major factors:
• The British had superior military technology and organization. This consisted notably in their possession of advanced firearms (especially the Maxim machine gun) and the navy. The latter gave them the ability to wage war from water-borne vessels. The combined effect of these was that British forces were able to fight from safe distances while inflicting heavy casualties on opposing armies.
• Indigenous political leaders failed to form alliances to pull their limited resources together and resist or frustrate the common enemy.

The result was that the British were able to recruit soldiers from one area to topple another, and to use intelligence gathered from one people against the other.

Once the peoples of the Niger and Benue areas were effectively brought under control, the British next set out to impose new political and economic systems necessary to achieve their purpose and mission.

The Sokoto Caliphate – Northern Nigeria

Founded between 1804 & 1809 by Uthman Dan Fodio, the Sokoto Caliphate overthrew and brought under one umbrella the warring, independent Hausa states via jihad or holy war. It was a religious state modeled after the one founded by the Islamic Prophet Mohammed in 7th Century Arabia.

The Caliphate was headed by a Caliph (Arabic word for "steward"). He wielded a combination of moral, political, military and religious authority, and was considered a successor (in faith) to Prophet Mohammed.

Dan Fodio was the first Caliph of Sokoto. When he retired from active duties, he handed over to his son Mohammed Bello and brother, Abdullahi. Each looked after a group of provinces. Afterwards, succession was not hereditary or by bloodline. Kingmakers selected from among close lieutenants and descendants of the first Caliph by considering their Islamic scholarship and moral standing.

Below the Caliph were the Emirs who led smaller political units called Emirates. Founded by "flag bearers" or lieutenants of Dan Fodio, the emirates were largely independent, but pledged allegiance and paid annual axes to the Caliphate. At the height of the Sokoto Caliphate, there were up to 30 emirates stretching as far south as Ilorin in the Northern fringes of Yoruba land. Below the Emirs were the Sarkis or town/community heads.

Land was communally owned and allocated equitably. Slaves who became Muslims automatically earned their freedom as Muslims could not enslave fellow Muslims. These reforms helped create a sense of social justice and drew many followers away from the decadent Hausa city states to the new Caliphate regime. It brought relative peace and stability to the territory for nearly 100 years.

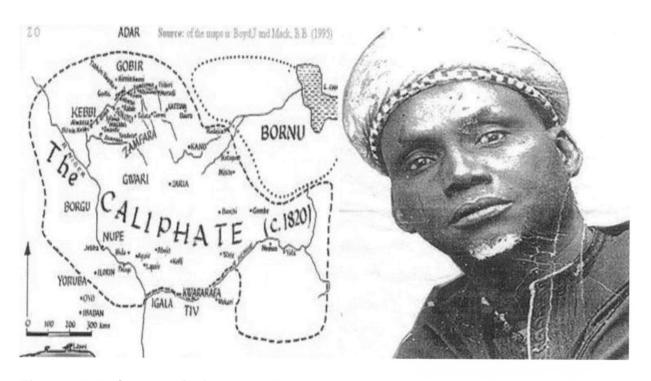

Figure 1: Sokoto Caliphate at the height of its power in the late 19th Century; (R) Undated portrait of Sheikh Uthman Dan Fodio. He lived between 1754 and 1817.

The Empire System of Oyo - Western Nigeria

Founded in the 15th Century by Oraminyan, one of the sons of Oduduwa, Oyo Empire lasted remarkably long until the late 19th century. Oyo's system of government could be described as constitutional monarchy, although the constitution was an un-written one.

At the head of the empire was the Oba (King) who took the title of Alaafin (meaning "owner of the palace"). He had enormous executive powers, but because custom forbade him from leaving the palace after coronation, he acted mostly through intermediaries. One of them was the First born Prince, Aremo.   There were also the feared royal messengers, the Alarin, who were half-shaved eunuchs.

The Alaafin position was not automatically handed down from father to son but was reserved for descendants of Oraminyan from the Ona Isokun royal ward. He was expected to be strong, fearless and war-like. Below the Alain was an advisory and legislative council of seven chiefs called the Oyo Mesi. Led by the Bashorun who also doubled as Aare Ona Kakanfo (Commander-in-Chief of the Army), the Oyo Mesi also had the power to select the Alaafin whenever there was a vacancy. And if the Alaafin committed an abomination or grievously lost favor, the Oyo Mesi also had the power to present him with a ritual calabash or parrot egg, upon which he must commit suicide.

Next to the Oyo Mesi was the Ogboni, a powerful society of free men who earned their status by age, wisdom, religious or social clout.

Headed by the Oluwo who had direct and unfettered access to the king, the Ogboni acted as the voice of the people.

The Oyo Mesi and Ogboni acted as checks and balances to the executive powers of the Alaafin as well as moderated the powers of one another. This was highly successful in checking tyranny and probably helps account for the longevity of the Oyo Empire. But there were several instances of abuse. The resultant instability eventually led to the decline and fall of this political edifice.

At the height of its power, Oyo had 4 administrative layers – Metropolitan Oyo, Yoruba Oyo, Egbado Corridor and Aja Land. Outside Metropolitan Oyo which was the nucleus of the empire, other vassal states were allowed significant autonomy as long as they paid taxes and tributes and owed allegiance to the central authority.

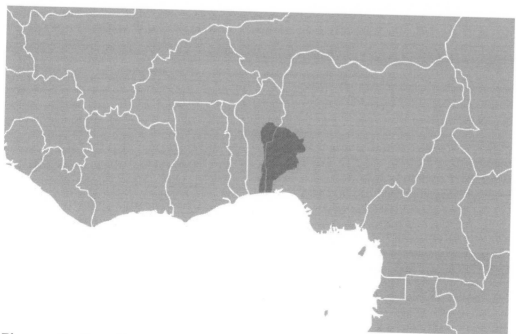

Figure 2: Oyo Empire extended to territories in present-day Nigeria and Benin Republic

The Republicans of Igboland - Eastern Nigeria

Pre-Colonial Igbo society was largely organized in small independent communities, each hardly more than the size of a town or city. Each town was made up of compounds (a collection of families), several of which formed villages. Groups of villages traced to a common ancestor formed clans. Several clans came together to form a town.

Although the political systems varied in detail from one area to another, they had two things in common:

(i) A strong sense of egalitarianism in which almost everyone was viewed as equal; no one was forbidden to wield power or influence; and individual accomplishment (not blood or ancestry) was the primary means of social and political promotion.

(ii) A deep respect for elders. Igbos widely correlated age with experience and wisdom, therefore elders were revered and their counsel rarely ignored. The oldest man in each compound, village or clan was widely consulted in customary matters and therefore occupied a quasi-political office.

At the head of each town was an Eze, Igwe or Obi. Although these titles translate to "King" or "Ruler", in reality their holders were far from imperial monarchs. With the exception of Onitsha, Oguta & some other Igbo communities west of the Niger (whose leadership were closer to monarchy), they were more or less administrators whose powers were severely limited by several institutions. These included:

- Ndi Ichie or Ndi Nze - The Council of Chiefs. Members of this council had advisory, judicial and religious roles all rolled into one.

In some areas, the council was headed by the Onowu – a traditional prime minister who was next in rank to the Eze.

- Next to the council of chiefs were various Age Grades and Associations. These acted as pressure groups and were frequently consulted before important decisions were reached. In matters of great public interest, the Eze could discretionarily summon the Oha n'Eze (Literally, "The people and the King" or General Assembly.) This gathering could be attended by all adult male and female citizens and free speech was guaranteed. Decisions reached at this assembly were final and binding.

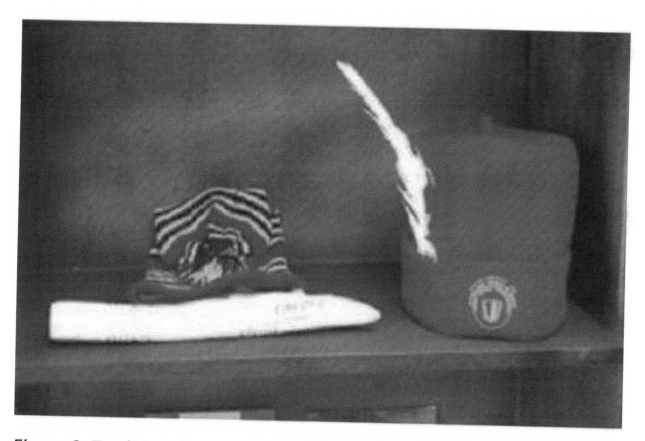

Figure 3: Traditional Igbo male head gears used by adult men (Left) and titled people (Right)

Chapter 2: Colonial Administration in Nigeria

The Purpose of Colonialism

Economic

The primary purpose of British colonial administration in Nigeria was to gain access and control over key economic activities of the area.

Following the abolition of the Trans Atlantic Slave Trade in the mid 19th Century, Britain (like France, Belgium, Spain & Portugal) needed cheap agricultural and mineral resources from around the world to feed her growing industrial complex. These included timber, cocoa, tobacco and palm produce from West Africa.

The forced annexation of Lagos in 1861 during the reign of Oba Dosunmu was aimed at taking over its important deep sea port through which much of the region's exports were shipped. Thus Lagos became the first part of Nigeria to be colonized – a victim of its own strategic location and economic importance. Other parts of Southern and Northern Nigeria followed between 1861 and 1898. Finally, the Sokoto Caliphate of Northern Nigeria was conquered in 1904 by an expeditionary force led by Fredrick Lugard.

Political

A second reason for British colonial involvement was political. It became a status symbol in Europe at the time for powerful nations with naval capabilities to "gain overseas territories" and dominate other nations. The scramble for and partition of Africa as well as other parts of the world was the direct result of this craze. The concept of "British Empire" was founded on this thirst for global prestige and dominance - Just as the rich desire to own lands and other properties.

Cultural & Ideological

As Britain, France and other European nations with strong navies grabbed territories around the world, they encountered resistance. They began to see the limits of military power and the need to win the hearts of colonized peoples in order to establish control. The British decided to send missionaries and administrators who introduced schools, hospitals and churches. The people were attracted by the services rendered by these institutions, notably in the areas of healthcare and literacy. Gradually, they were drawn into Western education, medicine, religion and political beliefs. The logic was simple: If you control their minds, you can control their government and economy indefinitely.

Figure 4: Illustration of European ships conducting business in a colonized territory

Figure 5: The scramble for Africa was to satisfy Europe's quest for dominance using force

Types of Colonial Administration

There were three main types of colonial administration operated by the British - Protectorates, Crown Colonies and Colonies.

Protectorates

A protectorate is an independent state or political unit which has signed an agreement with Britain to establish a partnership for "mutual benefit." Usually, in ex-change for free access to local markets and a guarantee of safety for British merchants, such states were promised the military "protection" of British forces in the event of attack by rival or neighboring states. This was usually the first form of intervention by Britain in the political and economic affairs of other nations.

Crown Colonies

When protectorate status was not enough to guarantee British commercial and other interests, they usually introduced Crown Colonies. These were territories over which the British monarch appointed a Governor to supervise British interests. The governors had legislative and administrative powers and reported only to the British Crown. They were usually chosen from the licensed agent company operating in the area, in Nigeria's case, the Royal Niger Company. The effect of having a British appointed "governor" operating in an "independent" state is that the powers of the local political authorities were compromised.

Any decisions which had potential impact on British citizens and interests had to be discussed and "cleared" with the governors. Local chiefs effectively lost their independence for a partnership status.

Colonies

These were territories or states which had come under the full, direct control and influence of the British government. Their chiefs and other political authorities had surrendered to foreign rule, usually under a Governor-General appointed by the Colonial Office. The Governor General made laws and ran the government. Local political authorities were only used as instruments of control over the natives.

In this stage, the British government bypassed the agent company it earlier licensed (Royal Niger Company) and took direct political and administrative control. This enabled it to deploy more resources (notably military and political) to protect British national interests, especially against competition from rival colonial nations like France, Belgium and Germany who were active on the continent. The British government eventually paid off the Royal Niger Company for its services.

Figure 6

Instruments of Colonial Administration

British colonial rule over Nigeria was established and maintained using a combination of instruments including treaties, force, taxation and cultural re-orientation. The latter was achieved through the introduction of Christianity and Western Education.

Treaties

These were the first instruments used to gain some form of colonial domination. hey were "agreements" written or drafted by agents of the colonizing power, supposedly in the name of the British Crown, which leaders of independent states were coaxed to sign, establishing a relationship with Britain. Since the treaties were in English and the native signatories were almost always not literate in the language, such agreements were in fact and by law flawed if not fraudulent. But they were often imposed by force or threat of force as was the case in Lagos under Oba Dosunmu.

Force

Sometimes, when a native authority would not succumb to intimidation, the British used direct military power to overthrow sovereign states and take over control. This was the case in Bini Kingdom and Sokoto Caliphate which were conquered in 1897 and 1904 respectively. Because traditional African societies did not possess firearm technology, they were easily defeated by small British forces wielding rifles, machine guns and cannons. Apart from their long-range and devastating impact, the explosive sounds of these weapons were unknown and helped demoralize local forces.

Taxation

After some time, particularly following the end of World War 1, the British began to find it difficult to finance colonial operations. They decided that each colony would raise revenues locally to support its administration. One way to do this was to levy taxes on natives. Laws were enacted requiring adult males to pay taxes and collecting portions of their earnings from economic activities. This was a new and offensive experience for most natives. It inadvertently laid the foundation for mass resistance (like the Aba Women's riot of 1928) which eventually led to calls for independence.

Religion & Western Education

Apart from force, by far the most effective instruments of colonialism were the twin tools of religious and intellectual conversion. The British first came as Christian missionaries offering conversion to a new faith. When this didn't work, they added the "gift" of Western education and medicine. Thus, the first schools and hospitals were built beside churches. The schools taught the basic skills of reading, writing and arithmetic. In a region where literacy was almost non-existent, this soon became a hit.

The first natives to learn to read, write and speak the English language became privileged members of society and role models. They were engaged as teachers, catechists and interpreters. Soon, everyone wanted to send their children to school to learn "the Whiteman's ways." Once intellectually and spiritually compromised, colonialism became easier – at least for some time. But in the long run, Christianity and Western education also became instruments for the dismantling of colonialism.

Figure 7: Itshekiri chiefs meeting with a British official

Figure 8: British soldiers and their African recruits firing at natives from the safety of small naval canoes

Figure 9: Unidentified European teaching young Africans how to read and write

Key Colonial Policies

Indirect Rule

Instead of hiring and paying new officials to do the work of administering local peoples, the British simply continued to use existing administrative structures and persons - as long as they were subservient. For example, the Obas in the West and the Emirs in the North became appendages of British rule. In the South-East where there were no comparable structures, the British created "Warrant Chiefs" to play the role. The chiefs thus became intermediaries between their own peoples and the colonial overlords – at almost no expense to British taxpayers.

This was very convenient since the British neither had enough men nor money to go round. Nor did they understand the cultures of the peoples well enough to govern them directly. This was a smart, simple and cost-effective tool of colonialism. The author of British Indirect Rule in colonial Africa was Sir Fredrick Lugard, although the principle of indirect rule has been used by colonial powers throughout history.

Figure 10

Divide & Rule

Closely related to the British colonial policy of Indirect Rule was the policy of Divide and Rule. The British realized early in their colonial experience that they were a small nation spread thin across the globe by their imperial ambitions; and that if any cluster of the diverse peoples they subjugated managed to unite under one banner, they (the British) stood little chance of maintaining their grip. Therefore, they devised the policy of discreetly playing one group against the other in order to keep them perpetually suspicious of one another and unable to form a common front against colonial domination.

In Nigeria, this took the form of regionalism. The concept of North, East and West was a British creation and did not exist prior to the colonial period. By rigorously pursuing a policy of "Separate Development", the British deliberately emphasized the differences between the diverse peoples of Nigeria, instead of building a common sense of nationhood along the lines of the Amalgamation. Each region was encouraged to "grow at its own pace."

One of the grossly under-reported aspects of British rule in Nigeria was the role played by colonial officials and intelligence agents in exacerbating the conflicts between Nnamdi Azikiwe, Obafemi Awolowo and Ahmadu Bello during the struggle for Nigeria's independence. It is instructive to note, for instance, that both the *Egbe Omo Oduduwa* (Association of the children of Oduduwa) and the *Jamiyar Mutanen Arewa* (Association of Northerners) were formed abroad by Nigerian students in the UK for further education. Their studies were almost always "sponsored" by the British colonial government. The cultural groups they formed, which eventually transformed into political parties, were clearly regional and parochial. It is easy to deduce that these organizations were remotely programmed to achieve a certain end. The real goal of British officials was to checkmate the growing influence of the NCNC under Herbert Macaulay, Nnamdi Azikiwe and others who were fiercely radical and anti-British.

The policy of divide and rule was also visibly at play on the floor of the Nigerian parliament during the 1953 motion for Independence debate. Northern parliamentarians were advised to vote against early independence because the region did not have enough educated elite to fill plum vacant posts in the event of British exit. This ploy was used to defer independence and extend colonial rule by a few years. Meanwhile, it was the British who for years pursued a policy of deliberately "starving" the North of Western education in order to maintain the grip of the Emirs on the people. The idea of three separate "nations" within a nation gradually stuck and Nigeria has carried on with it ever since, even creating more "nations."

Figure 11

Economic Dependency

This was another major policy plank on which British colonial rule rested. It means that the British reconfigured the key economic activities of the territory to rely almost exclusively on the needs and convenience of the British economy. The colony was forbidden from trading freely with any country except Britain. Thus, only cocoa, timber, groundnuts, oil palm, rubber and other major export crops needed by British industries were encouraged. Their prices were also determined and fixed in London.

These prices were far from competitive or fair. They were fixed to help British industries maximize their profits. They were only enough to keep the farmers interested and in the farms – not to prosper or grow in any meaningful way. When demand for colonial produce fell in the UK, prices and markets crashed here. When demand rose in the UK, prices rose only sluggishly here. In effect, the economy of Nigeria and the livelihood of Nigerians under colonial rule were entirely in British hands. This was an indirect form of enslavement.

Figure 12

Slow & Gradual Self-Rule

By the time the Second World War ended in 1945, peoples in the colonies had seen the British for who they truly were – a highly manipulative people. Almost with one voice, they began demanding for independence. Britain was economically and militarily too weak to fight and decided on a policy of slow and gradual self-rule for colonies. This was to give her enough time to:

- Quickly milk colonial economies to rebuild her own.
- Come up with a program by which Britain continues to benefit even after the colonies gain independence
- Negotiate a dignified exit.

In the end, Britain was able to buy another 15 years to wind down her colonial operations in Nigeria which eventually ended in 1960.

Figure 13

Key Colonial Personalities

Apart from Miss Flora Shaw (later Mrs. Flora Lugard), a journalist who gave Nigeria its name in an article she wrote for **The Times** in 1897, other leading British personalities in Nigeria's colonial experience were mostly Governors General who administered the country. They set the tone for socio-political development through their policies, leadership styles and the various constitutions they enacted which bore their names.

There were a total of 8 colonial Governors General of Nigeria between 1914 and 1960. Each spent an average of 5 years. Three (Donald Cameron, Graeme Thompson and Bernard Bourdillon) were in office during the great depression years and the Second World War which followed. Perhaps as a result, they were largely inconspicuous.

In this section, we shall highlight the key contributions of the remainder 5 to Nigeria. Plus another British personality who played a notable role in Nigeria's political development but was not its governor - Oliver Lyttelton. He was Secretary of State for the Colonies who revised the Macpherson Constitution and provided the last framework under which Nigeria finally gained independence.

Figure 14: Mrs. Flora Lugard (Nee Shaw). She suggested the name Nigeria (from Niger area) in an article written as a reporter on colonial affairs. Later married Nigeria's first Governor General.

Sir Fredrick Lugard

Figure 15: Sir Frederick Lugard, Founder & Commander of West African Frontier Force; First Governor General of Amalgamated Nigeria

He was the poster boy of British colonial rule in Nigeria and perhaps West Africa. Born to British parents in India in 1858, he was a soldier, mercenary, explorer and colonial administrator. He served as founder and commander of the West African Frontier Force (WAFF), in Northern Nigeria as High Commissioner and Hong Kong as Governor before returning to Nigeria in 1912 as Governor of both the Southern and Northern Protectorates.

In 1902, he married Miss Flora Shaw, a writer for The Times of London who coined the name Nigeria. He brought Northern Nigeria effectively under British rule by leading successful military expeditions against Kano and Sokoto in 1903.

One of his most memorable contributions was to oversee the Amalgamation of the Northern and Southern protectorates into a single colony in 1914. He became its first Governor General until 1919. The primary motive for amalgamation was administrative. At that time, revenues from the North were not enough to cover the cost of governance. Meanwhile, revenues from the South (essentially from liquor tax) were surplus. By merging the two, Lugard could pull resources together and deploy on the basis of need without breaching administrative procedures. It was also possible to reduce the overall size and cost of bureaucracy needed to govern the entire area.

His enduring intellectual contribution was the book, ***The Dual Mandate in British Tropical Africa*** (published 1922) in which he boldly outlined his views and justifications for British imperialism.

Sir Hugh Clifford

Figure 16: Sir Hugh Clifford: Set up Nigeria's first legislative council with provision for 4 elected indigenous representatives. This opened the way for the emergence of the earliest modern political parties.

The son of a British Army General who chose to go into the civil service, Sir Hugh succeeded Lugard as colonial Governor of Nigeria between 1919 and 1925. His were 7 largely uneventful years, the sole bright light of which was the Constitution of 1922. It set up a new Legislative Council of 46 members for the Southern Protectorate only (ignoring the North). This established the elective principle for the first time in Nigeria. Twenty seven (27) members of the council were drawn from officials of government while 19 were unofficial members. Of the nineteen unofficial members, ten (10) were Nigerians; 4 elected (3 for Lagos and 1 for Calabar). The rest 6 were appointed.

Under the Clifford constitution, the right to vote and be voted for was limited to adult males with annual in-come of up to 100 pounds. The need to fill the 4 elective positions made way for the establishment of Nigeria's first political parties, starting with Herbert Macaulay's Nigerian National Democratic Party (NNDP) in 1923.

Clifford's heart was however neither in Nigeria nor in Africa but in Malaya where he started his career and spent many of his early years. He wrote several fond stories, reflections and novels about his experience there, but little about Nigeria.

Sir Arthur Richards

Figure 17: Sir Arthur Richards: Expanded the central legislative council and created regional legislative councils for the first time.

Born in Bristol, England, in 1885, he married Miss Noelle Whitehead in 1927. He served as British colonial governor of North Borneo, Gambia, Fiji and Jamaica before his posting to Nigeria between 1943 and 1948.

His constitution of 1946 replaced and tried to improve on the Clifford Constitution of 24 years earlier. It included the North for the first time in the Nigerian Legislative Council and expanded popular participation by Nigerians in the law making process. Of the 44 members of his

Legislative Council, 28 (or 64%) were not serving officials of government. Twenty-four (24) of them were indirectly elected and 4 directly elected.

The Richards constitution also introduced regionalism into Nigerian politics by creating for the first time 3 regional legislative councils (one each for the North, East and West) with varying membership compositions. In addition, he created a Regional House of Chiefs for the North alone. In retrospect, this appears to have been part of the British policy of Divide and Rule which was designed to keep Nigerians distracted with internal disputes, thus slowing down agitation for self rule.

On face value, the Richards Constitution looked like a huge leap from the Clifford era. But it was not considered good enough by the Nigerian elite freshly motivated by the eye-opening experiences of World War II. Expectedly, it was highly criticized and condemned from the start. Richards was accused of not consulting the people before imposing a constitution on them. The NCNC embarked on a nationwide tour to galvanize public support for its cancellation and raise funds to send a protest delegation to London. This constitution was suspended in 1951, making it the most short-lived in colonial Nigeria.

Sir John Stuart Macpherson

Born in 1898 in Edinburgh, Scotland, he was educated at the University of Edinburgh. He joined the army but he was wounded in action during World War 1. After the war, he joined the civil service, serving in various posts around the world until he was appointed Governor of Nigeria in 1948.

The dust raised by the Richards Constitution was so much that he suspended it in 1950 and replaced it in 1951. The Macpherson Constitution created a new Council of Ministers which effectively opened the way for Nigerians to get involved in the central executive arm of government for the first time. It also expanded the central legislature by creating a House of Representatives with 185 members.

On account of these reforms, Macpherson is credited with creating the first "semi-responsible government" in colonial Nigeria. But despite strong arguments, he retained the regional councils, thus refusing to treat the country as a unified entity.

Oliver Lyttelton

Figure 18: Oliver Lyttleton: In his capacity as Secretary of State for Colonies, he amended the Macpherson constitution to increase indigenous participation in government and make the regions largely autonomous.

He was never Governor or Governor General of colonial Nigeria. But he earned his place in Nigerian history as Secretary of State for the Colonies from 1951 to 54. What came to be called the Lyttelton

Constitution of 1954 was actually a revision of the much-criticized Macpherson Constitution which he (Lyttelton) ordered in his capacity as Colonial Secretary.

Interestingly, it retained one of the most controversial elements – the un-identical regional councils and the principle of separate development (aka regionalism).

Lyttelton provided for a 184 member central House of Representatives with a speaker and 3 ex-officio members. He also provided for a 13 member federal Council of Ministers chaired by the Governor General, ten of them representing the various regions. Regional Houses of Assembly and Houses of Chiefs were created, except for the East which had only a House of Assembly.

His two most important contributions were:

(1) He expanded the space for indigenous participation in governance by providing for hundreds more positions to be filled by direct and indirect elections as well as by appointment. This covered the executive, legislative and judicial arms of government at both federal and regional levels.

(2) He introduced the concept of federalism by making the regional governments largely autonomous from the central government. It was the "final leap" towards independence.

Sir James Robertson

Figure 19: Sir James Robertson. He supervised the final handover of government to Nigerians at Independence.

He was the last British Governor of Nigeria and oversaw a controversial but peaceful handover of power to an independent government in 1960. Born in Dundee, Scotland, in 1899, he served the colonial office in Sudan for a long time. But it was his work in Guyana that earned him a posting to Nigeria as Governor General in 1955.

His major constitutional contribution was to supervise the preparation of the Independence Constitution which took effect from October 1, 1960. It provided for an independent, democratic government modeled after the British Parliamentary system. There was to be a bi-cameral (twin) federal legislature – The Senate and House of Representatives. In addition, three regional parliaments – one each for the East, West and North – were created. The Parties which won majority of seats in each parliament formed the government by nominating the Prime Minister or Premiers who became Heads of Government at federal and regional levels respectively.

To act as a check on the enormous powers of the Prime Minster, the position of Head of State was created. The Queen of England was named as titular Head of State, but was represented by the Governor General. In that capacity, Robertson remained as Governor General for a month and half after independence. On November 16, 1960, Nnamdi Azikiwe, took over from Robertson as Governor General, Head of State and representative of the Queen. It was not until the Republican Constitution of 1963 that Azikiwe was named President to replace the Queen as Head of State of independent Nigeria.

Years into retirement in 1974, Robertson wrote his highly acclaimed memoir, Africa in Transition: From Direct Rule to Independence, in which he reflected on his 4 decades of work in Africa and chronicled the challenges he and his fellow colonial civil servants faced in managing the disintegration of the once mighty British Empire.

Impact of Colonialism

The effects of 60 - 100 years of British colonial rule on Nigeria continue to be a controversial subject of discussion to this day. The consensus appears to be that it was a mixed bag of merits and demerits. Which one outweighs the other often depends on individual background and perspective. Below are some of the consequences.

Merits

1. Nigeria as a geo-political entity owes its creation entirely to British colonialism. Before the British arrived in pursuit of their own ambition, there was no nation called Nigeria. Several peoples, communities, chiefdoms, kingdoms and empires lived in the territory, independent of one another. But through military threats, brutal conquests, dubious treaties and suspicious administrative considerations, the world's largest Black nation was forged. And it remains one of the best hopes for an African re-birth.

2. Colonialism was the highway through which the peoples of Nigeria accessed Western education and culture and strengthened their foothold on the modern world. British explorers were followed by missionaries who offered Christianity and Western education to gain the confidence of the people.

Although it turned out to be a trap, the people ultimately gained knowledge of another way of life. In a sense, this continues to serve them well as no knowledge is lost. Christianity helped eliminate several negative beliefs and practices like animism and the killing of twins. Literacy helped improve sanitation, health and general standards of living.

3. Economically, new cash and export crops were encouraged by the British to meet their country's needs. In effect, agricultural production in Nigeria was raised from subsistence to mass production.

4. In the area of infrastructure, a modern transportation system was built with the construction of road and rail networks as well as sea ports and airports. A postal and telecommunications system was also introduced. All these helped the movement of people and economic resources as well as the efficient transmission of messages.

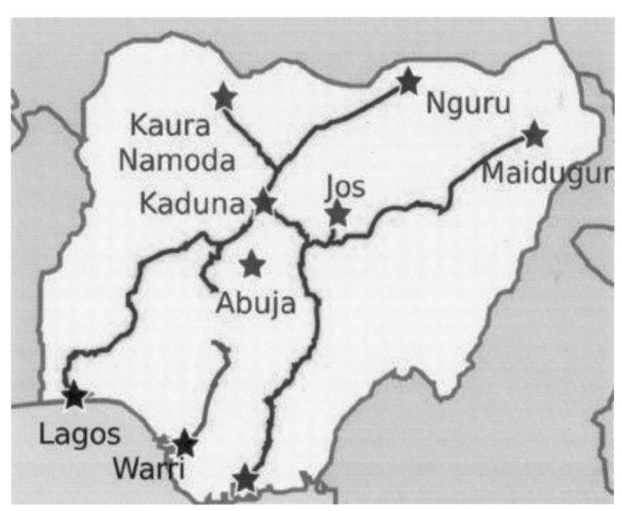

Figure 20: Map of Nigeria showing major rail networks. Most of these were constructed by the colonial government to evacuate produce and minerals from all over the country.

Demerits

1. Emotionally, colonialism was devastating to all its victims. The fact that the British conquered dominated and ruled our people without consent for years left many with low self esteem. Till date, some especially among the older generations which witnessed it, continue to feel inferior to the "White man."

2. Our cultures, traditions and value systems also got savaged. For example, Western dress codes more suited to the cold climate of Europe were adopted without much thought, even though it is not ideal for our tropical environment. Similarly, Western morals concerning sex, divorce and treatment of elders have in some places replaced superior traditional practices. Overall, Nigerians suffer from conflicts and confusion arising from that clash of cultures.

3. Economically, our country's mineral and agricultural resources were massively exploited for years to develop the British society. Our miners, farmers and soldiers worked tirelessly to earn paltry prices and wages determined in London. In some ways, this system of economic dependency and unfair trade practices has continued to this day.

4. Some say that the greatest negative impact of British rule has been in the area of politics. Colonial officers created regionalism and exploited the ethnic and linguistic differences of Nigeria to stay in power. They eventually handed over to Nigerian leaders who did not have the sense to dismantle those negative structures and build a truly united nation. The result has been unending mutual suspicion and political instability, sometimes leading to violence and war.

Figure 21: Colonialism was not just a mismatch of military technology. It also savaged the emotions, values and cultures of the colonized

Chapter 3: Rise of Nationalism

Nationalism – What does it Really Mean?

Nationalism simply refers to a feeling or sense of pride in one's country. Just as people feel proud and protective of their families, friends, schools and communities, so they may also feel about their countries. At times, this is because they have no other country, and it is natural to love and protect what belongs to us. At other times, it is because their country is big, powerful, successful, prosperous, protective or kind to them.

Nationalism may take any one or more of the following forms:
• Loyalty or devotion to one's country above loyalty to any other individual or group. This is called patriotism.
• Sovereignty or autonomy from any other country in the way it manages its affairs. This is commonly called independence.
• Belief that one's country is superior to another country in one way or another (size, economy, population, race, military power, etc), and therefore may exercise authority or influence over such country. This is called imperialism.

From a modern international relations point of view therefore, Nationalism has both positive and negative dimensions. Patriotism and Independence may be said to be its positive aspects while imperialism is clearly a negative form of nationalism – because it has a potential to lead to interference, aggression, war and other forms of conflict.

For Nigeria, nationalism first took the form of struggle for independence from colonial rule. Since independence was achieved, it has stayed alive mostly in the form of patriotism.

Figure 22

Causes of Nigerian Nationalism

It took a while for nationalist feelings to develop among the diverse peoples of Nigeria because the country did not exist before the British created it in 1914. Indeed, with the exception of the educated elites of Lagos and Calabar, most of the people were blissfully ignorant when Nigeria came into existence, how and why. The British system of Indirect Rule also ensured that most communities kept their old leaders and did not feel any significant changes in their lives or political status until well into the 1920s.

It took a number of events and developments before things changed and the fire of Nigerian nationalism began to burn.

1. Gradually, the people began to notice that their leaders were compromised and were no longer making decisions entirely in their interest. They observed that their leaders, who had dealings with the British and were receiving gifts and other forms of support from them, were becoming high-handed or detached from local reality. Lower ranked chiefs began to complain that they and traditional institutions like the council of chiefs and elders, were increasingly being ignored or bypassed as the British preferred to deal with a single authority in each major community. This led to a period of unease and clashes within traditional leadership institutions all over the country.

2. Soon after the end of World War 1 in 1918, the British were forced by economic difficulties to ask the colonies to raise revenues locally. Direct taxes were introduced for the first time in parts of Nigeria.

People felt their personal incomes and liberties affronted like never before. This sparked off popular discontent and eventually protests. The famous Aba Women's Riot of 1929 was one of such protests.

Figure 22: Aba Women's Riot

3. The violence with which these protests were put down added fuel to fire. People all over Nigeria began to feel the oppression of a foreign power. Soon, they realized the need for broader collective action beyond their immediate communities. They began to organize themselves into interest and pressure groups for self-defense and to fight a common enemy. The town and labor unions which began to spring up at this time became platforms for mobilization and seeds of future nationalist organizations.

4. The spread of Western education also played a part in the rise of Nigerian nationalism. The first generations of Western educated Nigerians were from the Lagos colony. After graduating from school, they realized that British people with equal or lower qualifications were given preferential treatment in job positions and pay. They soon began to agitate for fairer treatment, more opportunities and eventually equal treatment. The pattern was similar all across Nigeria. Such was the case with Herbert Macaulay, often called the father of Nigerian nationalism. When the Clifford Constitution of 1922 first provided for elected members of parliament, Nigeria's educated elites formed the first modern political party in the country, the Nigerian National Democratic Party (NNDP). Other parties like the Nigerian Youth Movement (NYM) followed.

These parties later began to mobilize people for mass action to press their demands. Nationalism was born.

5. The last major factor that led to the rise of Nigerian nationalism was the Second World War. When Germany under Adolf Hitler began attacking other countries of Europe in 1939, Britain ran to its African colonies for support to fight the Nazis. Support came in the form of men and materials. In Nigeria, young men were recruited from all over the country to fight on the side of the British Army. In the battlefields, they saw the British vulnerable, fearful and humble for the first time. By end of the war, the myth of British invincibility and superiority was broken for good. Soldiers returned from the war-fronts with greater sense of dignity and pride in their own abilities. Together with the politicians, the labor unions and the masses, they began to ask for equality, self rule and independence.

Figure 23: African resistance fighters

Figure 24: Outbreak of World War II helped expose and weaken the British Empire

Major Nationalist Leaders and Ideologies

Nigerian nationalism was a long and hard-fought struggle involving many individuals and groups over a long period of time. In a sense, it even predates the formation of the Nigerian state in 1914, to include all those brave men and women who resisted or fought the British in an attempt to maintain the independence of their territories – leaders like Oba Dosunmu of Lagos, King Jaja of Opobo, Oba Ovaremwen of Benin and Sultan Atahiru of Sokoto, among others.

But for the purpose of this work, we must limit our scope to the period of 1914 to 1960; and only to those who fought to dislodge British colonial rule after it had been formally established over the area called Nigeria.

Of the many characters involved, the following are widely believed to stand head and shoulders above the crowd:

1. Herbert Macaulay
2. Nnamdi Azikiwe
3. Obafemi Awolowo
4. Ahmadu Bello
5. Tafawa Balewa

Figure 25: Pre-Colonial Nigerian leaders who resisted British domination: Clockwise, Oba Ovaremwen of Benin with two of his queens; King Jaja of Opobo; and Sultan Atahiru of Sokoto. Ovaremwen & Jaja were exiled. Atahiru was captured and killed.

Herbert Olayinka Macaulay

Figure 26: Herbert Macaulay (1864 – 1946): Engineer, activist, pioneer politician & Father of modern Nigerian nationalism

Born in Lagos in 1864 by a Sierra Leonean father and a daughter of the famous Bishop Ajayi Crowther, he is widely recognized as the founder of modern Nigerian nationalism. He attended CMS Grammar School Lagos and studied both Engineering and Architecture in England. Upon his return in 1893, he worked as a surveyor with the colonial service but let after 6 years (allegedly over growing disaffection with colonial injustices) to go into private practice.

From that point on, he began to write articles in support of numerous indigenous rights causes, especially to fight unjust land acquisitions by the colonials. To further his interests, he co-founded the Nigerian Daily News, a platform he used to cement his place in Lagos social and political circles. When the Clifford Constitution provided the first opening for indigenous participation in legislative affairs, he founded the NNDP in 1923. It became the first Nigerian political party and won all the elective seats in the Lagos Town Council until 1933.

Macaulay's political fortune nose-dived after that following the rise of the Nigerian Youth Movement (NYM) and double convictions for fraud and sedition by an obviously alarmed colonial government. But in 1944, he pulled off a political resurrection by co-founding and leading the National Council of Nigeria and the Cameroons (NCNC). NCNC was the first Nigerian political organization with the goal of bringing together all parts of the country (including those which joined from Cameroon) to ask for independence. Macaulay died in 1946 following a sudden illness and leadership of the NCNC fell on Azikiwe, his trusted, younger lieutenant.

Dr. Nnamdi Azikiwe

Figure 27: Nnamdi Azikiwe (1904 – 1996); Journalist, media celebrity, orator and politician

Born in 1904 in Zungeru, present-day Niger State (Northern Nigeria) to Igbo parents from Onitsha (in Eastern Nigeria), Azikiwe spent his early life between Zungeru, Onitsha, Calabar and Lagos (Western Nigeria) where he attended Methodist Boys High School. As a result, he learnt to speak the Hausa, Igbo and Yoruba languages and became familiar with Nigeria's three major cultures. After a failed attempt to stow away in a US-bound ship, he worked briefly in Ghana as a policeman. Subsequently, his father raised enough money to send him to the USA for higher education. He studied politics, religion and anthropology at various universities and worked as a columnist and graduate student instructor before returning to Nigeria in 1934. Unable to find suitable work in Nigeria because of British discrimination against American degrees at the time, he moved to Gold Coast (Ghana) and resumed work as a journalist. He was a fierce Pan-Africanist in his writings, later starting the **West African Pilot** in 1937. This soon grew into a powerful group of newspapers.

By 1944 Zik was a media celebrity and teamed up with the highly experienced Herbert Macaulay to found the National Council of Nigeria and the Cameroons (NCNC). As a politician, he was a passionate nationalist who believed that all Nigerian groups without exception should unite against British rule and live as one. This ideology was probably inspired by his background, having grown up in different parts of the country, and by his expo-sure to American idealism. However, when his party lost the Western Regional majority due to cross-carpeting in 1951, he retreated to become Eastern Nigeria Premier in 1954. In the process, he dislodged Dr. Eyo Ita, a capable and loyal party man of Efik extraction.

This incident is believed to be at the root of Eastern minority distrust of the Igbo to this day. Zik's reputation as a nationalist never fully recovered from that move. He became Governor General of Nigeria in 1960 and President of the Federal Republic in 1963 - both roles being largely ceremonial. He was forced out of office in 1966 following Nigeria's first military coup. Subsequent attempts at leading Nigeria in 1979 and 83 failed. He died in Enugu in 1996. He is widely considered an idealist who was unable to bring his best ideas to life.

63

Chief Obafemi Awolowo

Figure 28: Chief Obafemi Awolowo (1909 - 1987); Teacher, lawyer, organizer, opposition leader and astute administrator

Born in Ikenne, Western Nigeria, in 1909, he studied at Wesley Teachers College, Ibadan and later trained as a lawyer at the University of London As a young man, he joined the radical Nigerian Youth Movement (NYM) in the 1930s. Together with others, he founded *Egbe Omo Oduduwa* in London shortly after the end of World War 2. This gave rise to Action Group (AG) in 1951. He led both organizations.

In 1951, after the NCNC won majority seats in Lagos and Azikiwe was set to emerge as head of government, Awo is said to have masterminded a mass desertion of NCNC parliamentarians to his party by appealing to ethnic sentiments against allowing a non-Yoruba (Zik) to lead them. This incident is believed to mark a watershed in the history of ethnic politics in Nigeria, with effects spiraling to this day.

As Premier of Western Nigeria from 1952 – 59 however, Awolowo is widely adjudged to have been an exceptional administrator, introducing welfare innovations like free education and running a highly efficient government. Ideologically, Awo was a Federalist (some say Regionalist) who believed that Nigeria was best served by largely autonomous regions, each looking after the needs of its own people.
In 1959, he became Leader of Opposition at the federal legislature. Firmly accomplished in Western Nigeria, Awo next attempted to move the AG from regional to national party. But he was firmly opposed by S.L. Akintola who took over from him as Premier. Awo accused Akintola of being an agent of the NPC / NCNC central coalition led by Prime Minister Tafawa Balewa, which he claimed wanted to neutralize the opposition. Akintola accused Awo of high-handedness and lack of democratic credentials.

The AG broke up in 1962 and violent crisis followed in Western Nigeria. Awo was jailed for treason and later released. Nigeria's First Republic never quite recovered from the chain of events that followed until it was sacked by a coup in 1966. Awo emerged as Finance Minister and trusted adviser of the Yakubu Gowon government which prosecuted the Nigerian Civil war. His attempts to lead Nigeria in 1979 and 1983 failed. His legacy is of a highly polarizing figure, widely hailed by many as a political and administrative genius and railed by others as a divisive influence and half-hearted nationalist.

Alhaji (Sir) Ahmadu Bello

Figure 29: Alhaji (Sir) Ahmadu Bello (1910 – 1966);
Teacher, grassroots mobilize and leader

Born in Rabah, near Sokoto, in 1910, he was educated at Katsina Training College and later became a teacher of English in Sokoto. He joined the local district administration in 1934, working his way up the ladder and earning a reputation as a skillful grassroots mobilizer. He travelled to Britain to study Local Government Administration in 1948, returning to serve as member of the Northern Regional House of Assembly. He was a member of *Jamiyya Mutanen Arewa* which later became the Northern People's Congress (NPC) in 1951.

A fearless defender of Northern interests, Ahmadu Bello became Premier of the region and party leader in 1954. In that position, he laid a solid foundation for the emergence of a united North. He was reputed to have very strong inter-personal and leadership skills which drew people to him. When NPC won the 1959 elections, he chose to remain as Premier, passing the role of Prime Minister to his deputy, Abubakar Tafawa Balewa.

His ideological convictions were clearly Regionalist. He believed that the peoples of Nigeria were naturally different and should be governed as such. He appeared to have nursed a deep suspicion about the Nigeria project, devoting all his energies to his beloved North. Given his almost entirely regional upbringing and limited metropolitan exposure, this is probably not surprising. It also helps explain his unusual decision to pass the opportunity to become Nigeria's first Prime Minister to his deputy, Tafawa Balewa, while remaining regional leader and kingmaker.

Bello was killed in Nigeria's first military coup in January, 1966. To the peoples of Nigeria's north, he remains a highly beloved son and pragmatist. To the rest of the country, he is largely seen as a regional and narrow-minded leader who declined to be a nationalist.

Alhaji (Sir) Tafawa Balewa

Figure 30: Alhaji (Sir) Tafawa Balewa (1912 – 1966);

He is rightly or wrongly seen as the last titan of Nigeria's Independence struggle and First Republic. Born in Bauchi, Northern Nigeria, in 1912, he studied at Barewa Teachers College and taught middle school for some time before proceeding to the University of London's Institute of Education in 1944. Upon return in 1946, he was appointed Inspector of Schools in the colonial service.

He was elected into the Northern House of Assembly in the same year and into the central Legislative Assembly in 1947 where he was an eloquent advocate of Northern interests. Along with Ahmadu Bello, he was one of the founding fathers of the Northern People's Congress (NPC). He served as Minister of Works and Minister of Transport between 1952 and 1957 and was reputed to have acquitted himself well as a manager of men. As Independence approached, he was appointed Chief Minister. Following the NPC's victory in the 1959 elections, he became Nigeria's first Prime Minister in 1960, forming a coalition government with the NCNC.

A quiet and humble man, Balewa was also a very intelligent and competent bureaucrat. But his tenure as PM was highly volatile as regional rivalry intensified and his every move was seen as regionally and remotely controlled by Ahmadu Bello and the NPC. He is widely blamed for lack of statesmanship and poor handling of the Western regional crisis of 1962 from which point the country slid into anarchy.

He died in the January 1966 military coup. He did not leave any major speeches or writings that define his national political ideology. It appears he was a natural technocrat whom fate thrust in the midst of fiery politicians and became a victim of their endless schemes.

Chapter 4: From Independence to Collapse of Civil Rule (1960 – 1967)

Highway to Anarchy

As the British flag (the union jack) was lowered and the green-white-green lag of newly independent Nigeria hoisted in its place on October 1, 1960, joy and optimism over-shadowed all other emotions. The people celebrated the end of colonialism and looked forward to the rise of an African power-house firmly in charge of its own destiny. The hope was that with Independence secured and governance in the hands of its own people, Nigeria would quickly overcome its numerous problems of nationhood, especially the divisive tendencies of its leaders and regions, evident from its anti-colonial struggle. Many also dreamed that it would emerge as a bastion of liberty and a pride to Black people.

But it did not take long before reality set in. The country's shoddy socio-political arrangements and weak inter-group foundations came back to haunt her. The first major sign of trouble occurred in May, 1962. It took the form of an open disagreement within the opposition AG between Chief Obafemi Awolowo, party and opposition leader in the Federal Parliament, and Chief Samuel Akintola, then deputy party leader and Premier of Western Nigeria.

Initial dispute centered on the fate and direction of the party. Awolowo wanted to transform the Action Group from a Western Regional party into a National movement with a radical socialist outlook and appeal to the youth. The goal was to build on its role as opposition party to create a more formidable platform capable of defeating the NPC and NCNC in subsequent elections. Akintola advocated that the Action Group should enter the Federal Coalition Government to stop the Yoruba from losing

Figure 38: Chief Obafemi Awolowo & Chief Ladoke Akintola: Their dispute over control of Action Group began the series of events that eventually led to the collapse of the First Republic

Figure 39: Street violence was rife as the government of Prime Minister Tafawa Balewa lost control

juicy appointments to rival ethnic groups. He argued that the Action Group should face reality and stay in the West. It was a battle between the purists and the pragmatists. This ideological difference spiraled into a personal conflict and struggle for power leading to the break-up of the AG into two factions. S.L. Akintola's Nigerian National Democratic Party (NNDP) emerged as splinter group.

Political crisis and violence erupted in the region-al parliament and on the streets of Western Nigeria. Prime Minister, Sir Abubakar Tafawa Balewa, declared a state of emergency in the Western Region. Dr. M.A. Majekodunmi was appointed Administrator. In 1963, at the expiration of the state of emergency, Akintola returned as Premier. In the elections of 1965, he won as candidate of NNDP which had entered into alliance with the ruling NPC!

All through the crisis, the AG cried foul, claiming the NPC was undermining it to gain control of the west. The NPC pleaded innocent, saying the AG imploded owing to internal ideological differences. The state of emergency was similarly seen in different lights. While the AG said it was designed to stop the party from properly removing the "mole" in its midst (Akintola) as premier and assuming rightful control of its western stronghold, the NPC claimed it was inevitable to halt further slide to anarchy. These series of events earned for the Western region the derisive appellation of "Wild, Wild, West."

At about the same time, the Census crisis of 1962 broke out. The exercise which commenced on May 13, 1962 was cancelled owing to allegations of widespread irregularity. Another attempt in 1963 was

Figure 40: Chief Ladoke Akintola in private discussion with Israeli Prime Minister, David Ben Gurion, during the former's visit to Israel about 1961

similarly discredited but officially accepted. With a total head-count of 55.6 million, each region and party accused the other of manipulating the exercise and cooking numbers for political advantage. Whilst opposition and census crisis simmered, Prime Minister Balewa decided in 1963 to carve out Mid-West Region from Western Region. Even though this was done under the pretext of agitation for self-determination and under the aegis of an all-party conference, it appeared hypocritical and intended to further weaken the opposition's political base as similar agitations in the North and East were blissfully ignored.

For instance, the peoples of the Middle Belt wanted out of the North while the peoples of Calabar-Ogoja-Rivers areas wanted out of the East. Yet none of these were granted regional status in 1964 alongside the Mid-West. To make matters worse, leading members of the opposition AG were arrested and put on trial over allegations of plotting to "forcefully overthrow the legitimate government in Nigeria."

If nothing else, the Federal Government under Prime Minister Tafawa Balewa and the NPC/NCNC alliance appeared guilty of administrative insensitivity and political naivety.

As political tension simmered, the lifestyle of politicians and public office holders grew more flamboyant. Festus Okotie-Eboh, who headed the Finance ministry, was particularly notorious for flashy and ostentatious displays. Suspicion and allegations of corruption became rife. Although rumors of impending military coup cropped up now and again, the politicians obviously did not take them too seriously.

Figure 41

Military Intervention in Politics

It was under such heavy clouds of political instability and moral disquiet that a group of young army officers struck on Saturday, January 15, 1966 in what became Nigeria's first military coup d'état. Led by Major Chukwuma Kaduna Nzeogwu, other key conspirators included Majors Timothy Onwuatuegwu, Emmanuel Ifeajuna, Adewale Ademoyega and Chris Anuforo. They were later called the Five Majors.

Disgruntled by the incompetence of the politicians, the young officers had ambitions of righting the wrongs of the time and putting the country back on track. According to Nzeogwu's noon speech made on Radio Kaduna, "The aim of the Revolutionary Council is to establish a strong, united and prosperous nation, free from corruption and internal strife. "

But like the people they sought to replace, the coupists lacked experience and political wisdom to implement their dreams. With the exception of Adewale Ademoyega, for instance, the rest of the coup leaders were officers of Igbo extraction. In a country where ethnic distrust was norm and the fear of "Igbo domination" had been part of the political lexicon since 1946, this was a major planning blunder. Team composition was unbalanced. To make matters worse, the emerging list of casualties, 11 senior politicians and 2 soldiers, contained no Igbo names! The Igbo members of the Balewa government were either safely out of the country (like Azikiwe), or

Figure 42: Major Chukwuma Kaduna Nzeogwu in a media interview before the coup of 1966

Figure 43: General J.T.U. Aguiyi-Ironsi: First Nigerian military Head of State, Jan. to July 1966

miraculously unharmed in the putsch!! Other ethnic groups cried foul. This was not just an implementation blunder; it turned out to be the major undoing of the coup. People, particularly from other ethnic groups, quickly concluded that the coup was a plot by Igbos to forcefully take over the country – something they could not do via the ballot box. This conspiracy theory gained ground. The 5 Majors had toppled a corrupt and inept government but lost the hearts of the people.

With little real control over combatant troops and the armory, the coup promptly failed. Its perpetrators either fled or were arrested. Remnants of the civilian government led by Senate President, Nwafor Orizu (who was Acting President in the absence of Azikiwe), announced a "voluntary" handover of power to the most senior Nigerian military officer, Major General Johnson Aguiyi-Ironsi.

Another account has it that Ironsi "at Gun point forced the remaining members of Balewa's Government to resign. He then made the Senate President Nwafor Orizu, who was serving as acting president in Azikiwe's absence, to officially surrender power to him, staging a coup of his own and ending the First Nigerian Republic."

Whatever the true account was, it turned out that the most senior military officer, Major General Johnson Aguiyi-Ironsi, was himself also Igbo. So, Ironsi took over government under heavy clouds of suspicion about his ethnicity, role in the coup and intentions. Simply put, the general was not trusted – neither within the army (his immediate constituency) nor among the people. With this dramatic turn of events, the political flash point suddenly shifted from Western to Eastern

Nigeria; from wild-wild-west to a deeply distrusted east. Disturbances in the west suddenly took a back seat as both North and West closed ranks at the prospect of a "conspiratorial" East. Over the next 6-7 months, Ironsi tried to stabilize the country through a series of administrative measures aimed at taking away power from the riotous regions and concentrating same in the hands of a more disciplined central government. This was encapsulated in his famous Decree No. 34.

It turned out to be an error of judgment. Subsequent events showed that the regions resented the idea of taking instructions for everyday business from a central government, especially one led by a man whose real loyalty or sympathy was in doubt. Ironsi also tried to court aggrieved ethnic groups through political appointments and patronage. But his failure to punish the coup plotters heightened suspicions about his complicity.

On July 29, 1966, 194 days after he became head of state, Ironsi was abducted from Government House, Ibadan. He was on a nationwide tour. His abductors were soldiers led by Theophilus Danjuma. His body and that of his host governor, Lt-Col Adekunle Fajuyi, were later found in a nearby forest. It was Nigeria's second coup, a counter coup led by officers of Northern extraction, who bought into the earlier Igbo conspiracy theory.

The original goal of the counter-coup led by Muritala Mohammed was to take the North out of Nigeria. "Araba", a word meaning "to separate", was not only the dominant slogan in the north at the time but also the code name for the July 1966 counter-coup. But through the combined effort of intellectuals, civil servants and emissaries of foreign governments, the secession element of the agenda was dropped. The coup leaders were persuaded that the overall best interests of the North were well served within a single country.

Figure 44: General T. Y. Danjuma: One of the principal leaders of the July 1966 coup and a leading member of military regimes throughout the 1970s

Chapter 5: The Civil War (1967-1970)

Background

Lt-Col Yakubu Gowon, Ironsi's former Chief of Army Staff, took over as Head of State in July 1966. Though not among the arrowheads of the counter-coup, his background as a Northerner who was neither Hausa-Fulani nor Muslim made him a safe choice to lead a nation soaked in ethnic and religious suspicion, especially among its major ethnic and religious groups. Gowon was Christian and Angas, an ethnic group from the Plateau area of North-Central Nigeria.

One of Gowon's earliest moves was to repeal Aguiyi-Ironsi's unitary decree and restore the federal structure of government with four regions. Reprisal attacks broke out in the Northern and Western parts of the country as soldiers of Northern origin attacked and killed their colleagues of Igbo or Eastern extraction in apparent revenge for the lopsided killings of the January coup. Hundreds died. The scene soon spilled into the streets where easterners were randomly mobbed and killed. Their shops and businesses were looted or razed. Gowon's government was largely ineffective in stopping this.

Thousands of Igbos and others from south-eastern Nigeria were murdered throughout the country in what came to be called a pogrom. Bodies littered the streets of Northern and Western Nigeria. Corpses were loaded on trains and shipped to the East. The arrival of such trains caused great revulsion among survivors and relatives. Over a million Igbos and other peoples of the East led towards their ancestral homeland.

Figure 45: Colonel Yakubu Gowon & Colonel Emeka Ojukwu: Led the country to civil war between 1967 and 1970

Figure 46: Ojukwu (2nd Let) & Gowon (2nd Right) in a group photograph with General Joe Ankrah (Middle) at Aburi, Ghana, in 1967

Lieutenant Colonel Chukwuemeka Odumegwu Ojukwu, military governor of the Eastern Region, assumed the role of Igbo leader by default. He argued that if Igbo lives could not be preserved by the Nigerian state, then the Igbo reserved the right to establish a state of their own in which their rights would be respected.

Aburi Accord

As tension rose between the Eastern Region and the Federal Government, Ojukwu asked for talks on "neutral soil" to discuss the thorny issues and agree a way forward. He said his safety and that of his delegation could not be guaranteed in any other part of Nigeria in an atmosphere of violence. The Aburi (Ghana) Summit of January 4-5, 1967 was proposed by then Ghanaian Head of State, Lt-General Joe Ankrah, in response. The Aburi Accord was the out-come. Till date, the exact content and meaning of the Aburi agreements remain a subject of controversy.

The controversy appears to revolve around interpretation of the following issues contained in the summit report:

1. National Governance
- "Members agreed that any decisions affecting the whole country must be determined by the Supreme Military Council. Where a meeting is not possible such a matter must be referred to Military Governors for comment and concurrence.
- Members agreed that "all the decrees passed since January 15, 1966, and which detracted from previous powers and positions of

regional governments, should be repealed if mutual confidence is to be restored."

2. Military Command Structure

• "Army to be governed by the Supreme Military Council under a chairman to be known as Commander-in-Chief of the Armed Forces and Head of the Federal Military Government.

• Establishment of a Military Headquarters comprising equal representation from the Regions and headed by a Chief of Staff.

• Creation of Area Commands corresponding to existing Regions and under the charge of Area Commanders.

▪ During the period of the Military Government, Military Governors will have control over Area Commands for internal security."

3. Return of Military Personnel to their Regions of Origin

• "Council reaffirmed the principle that Army personnel of Northern origin should return to the North from the West. In order to meet the security needs of the West it was agreed that a crash programme of recruitment and training was necessary but that the details should be examined after the Military Committee had finished its work."

While the Eastern delegation believed that the above agreements, taken together, amounted to "establishing Nigeria as a confederation of regions", the Federal side said nothing was farther from the truth. Confederation would have been Ojukwu's minimum target, given the widespread desire within the Eastern heartland at that time to be left alone to nurse its wounds. It would have been one step away from secession.

A confederation is "a union of sovereign states, united for purposes of common action often in relation to other states. " "Whereas a federation has a strong central government, a confederation is more of an agreement between separate bodies to cooperate with each other."

With agreements to return to the regional structure before Jan 1966; create military area commands under the control of regional governors; and have military personnel return to their home regions, Nigeria would have become a *de facto* confederation.

It would appear that the federal delegation was not fully aware of these implications until they returned home to Nigeria. Obviously after further reflection and consultations, Gowon issued the following press statement:

"We reviewed the situation in the Nigerian Army and we all agreed that there should be one Nigerian Army under a unified command as at present. We recognized that in the context of the events of 1966, the most practical way of achieving this aim is to organize the Army into area commands. The preponderance of the army personnel in each command will be drawn from the indigenes of that area. Each area command will be under an Area Commander who will take operational instructions from the Military Headquarters which will be directly under me as the Supreme Commander of the Armed Forces. Under the proposal, the Military Governors can use the area command for internal security purposes but this will normally be done with the express permission of the Head of the Federal Military Government. We definitely decided against Regional armies."

The Eastern side cried foul, claiming Gowon had made a "volte-face on solemn agreements." Over the next four months, tension rose to fever pitch across the country.

Figure 47: Street violence, mob killings and looting were rife all over the country as the federal military government failed to control inter-ethnic clashes

Figure 48: Biafrans fleeing their homes as shooting war began in July 1967

On May 5, 1967, Gowon abolished the 4 regions and created 12 states in their place. His aim was to weaken the hold of the major ethnic groups on regional and national governments by giving some minorities within each region their own states and therefore more say within the federal structure.

Three states came out of the former Eastern region - East-Central, South-Eastern and Rivers States. Gowon reasoned that the other ethnic groups of Eastern Nigeria would not actively support the Igbo cause if they were offered their own states. In essence, any breakaway effort for the entire east would be weakened, the Igbos isolated and more easily dealt with. He was right. This was a political master-stroke; a page from the tactical manuals of the former British colonial government.

Biafran Secession & Outbreak of War

On 30 May 1967, Ojukwu responded by declaring the formal secession of the Eastern Region, which was now to be known as the Republic of Biafra. This followed the resolution of a peoples' assembly held in Enugu at which the people expressed their loss of faith in Nigeria and their desire for a separate country.

Gowon mobilized federal troops to stop this. Alongside a military effort, he launched a propaganda campaign with the message: "To keep Nigeria one is a task that must be done." On the Biafran side, Ojukwu responded in kind: "Whoever is surrounded by enemies guards his life with all he has."

Civil war raged for thirty months, starting July 6, 1967 and ending January 15, 1970.

Figure 49: Nigerian artillery unit under the command of Col. Benjamin Adekunle (2nd Right) during the civil war

The most conservative estimates have it that well over a million lives were lost. Some say up to six million. Most of the casualties were on the Biafran side. The leading cause of death was not combat action but hunger, malnutrition and starvation. This was caused not just by severe dislocation of economic activities but also by encirclement and blockade of Biafra by federal forces, thus preventing both imports and delivery of international humanitarian assistance.

Militarily, Biafra stood no chance. It had no trained army, no significant armory and no major power behind it. Conversely, Nigeria had a standing army, the bulk of national defense capabilities and the support of both Britain and the Soviet Union. It was carnage unprecedented on the African continent at that time.

In accepting Biafra's unconditional surrender, Gowon magnanimously declared that there would be "No Victor, No Vanquished." In this spirit, the years afterward were declared to be a period of "rehabilitation, reconstruction and reconciliation."

Sadly, despite a sharp rise in national economic fortunes after the war following a period of oil boom, some of these slogans never let the drawing board. Partly as a result, the Eastern region witnessed high levels of misery, looting and armed robbery for years after the guns fell silent.

Figure 50: Biafran Kwashiokor victims. Millions of children like these died of starvation and malnutrition during the war

Chapter 6: Constitutional Developments (1963 – 1999)

Introduction

Major constitutional developments in Nigeria from the colonial period to independence have already been summarized under the biographies of the governors who introduced them (See section on Key colonial players in part 2). This section will provide narrative discussion only of post-independence constitutional changes. To wrap it all together, we will show a table capturing in a snapshot all the key constitutional changes and reforms from colonial times to 1999.

Figure 31: Nigeria's National Assembly complex, Abuja

First Republic Constitution – 1963

This was identical to the Independence (or Robertson) Constitution of 1960 in all respects except one: It removed the Queen of England as Nigeria's titular head of state. With this, the office of Governor General which represented the Queen was abolished. It was replaced by the office of President and Head of State. This was a largely ceremonial position as the Prime Minister was Head of Government and held real executive powers.

The concept and term "Republic" connotes that both constitution and government derive their powers and authority solely from the people – not from any individual, king, queen or foreign power. It signals independence and sovereignty.

In practice, Nigeria's First Republic Constitution was chaotic. There were numerous instances of strife beyond the normal conflicts of legislative conduct. Parliament became a theatre for individual, party and regional showdowns as members failed to play their role as statesmen and custodians of the peoples will. Not surprisingly, they were largely ineffective in checking the excesses of the executive arm of government.

This Constitution was suspended in January 1966 following the first military coup led by Major Chukwuma Kaduna Nzeogwu. For the next 13 years, Nigeria was governed through military decrees which were promulgated to serve the interests of the juntas with no inputs from the people.

Figure 32

Second Republic Constitution –1979

Introduced by the military government of General Olusegun Obasanjo, this constitution attempted to reflect the lessons learnt from the failure of the first Republic as Nigeria made another attempt at civil democracy. It replaced the British-style parliamentary system of government with the American multi-party presidential system.

To avoid the complications of the earlier parliamentary system which had both a Prime Minister and a President in office at the same time, this constitution provided for the office of (Executive) President. He or she was to be directly elected by the people – not by the majority party in parliament. The same applied to the governors of states (which replaced the regions).

It maintained the bi-cameral structure of the National Assembly by keeping the Senate and House of Representatives. Each state was however to have a single chamber State Assembly. It kept the federal structure of Nigeria as comprising of partially self-governing states under a central or federal government.

This constitution was in operation for only four years until December 31, 1983 when it was suspended following a military coup led by Generals Muhammadu Buhari and Tunde Idiagbon.

Figure 33: General Olusegun Obasanjo during his first tenure as Head of State in the late 1970s

Figure 34: Alhaji Shehu Shahari, Second Republic President, addressing a campaign rally

Figure 35: General Ibrahim Babangida, years after leaving office as Head of State and self-declared president

Third Republic Constitution – 1993

This constitution was actually drafted in 1989. It came into partial effect, with plans to become fully operational by 1993. But it never did. Introduced by General, Ibrahim Babangida, its main difference with the 1979 Constitution was that it abolished the multi-party system in favor of a two-party system. Most other elements of the two constitutions were identical.

Babangida observed that most successful democracies revolved around two major ideologies – one conservative and the other radical. He also observed that Nigerian political parties were not ideologically driven but always revolved around major ethnic groups or regions, thus dividing the country along its major fault lines. He reasoned that if all Nigerian politicians and political parties were forced to align themselves between the two main ideologies, the problem of ethnic or regional politics would be solved and the country would eventually embrace the proven ideological path to progressive democracy.

Babangida was perhaps intellectually right. But in practice he sabotaged his own plans by cancelling the 1993 presidential election won by the SDP's Moshood Abiola. In the mass uproar that followed, the Third Republic Constitution became inoperable. Babangida was forced to hand over power to an interim national government under Ernest Shonekan. Sonekan's task was to find a new way forward for the country but he was ousted in a military coup six months after by General Sani Abacha. Abacha had no real plans of relinquishing power until he died in office in 1998.

Fourth Republic Constitution – 1999

Introduced by General Abdulsalami Abubakar who took over from Sani Abacha on the latter's demise, this constitution is a replica of the 1979 Constitution.

It re-adopts the American Presidential system with an executive president, a bi-cameral central legislature, state governors and single-chamber state legislatures; all positions to be filled via direct elections contested in multi-party elections. It also upholds the federal structure of the Nigerian state and guarantees basic individual or citizen rights.

Figure 36: General Abdulsalami Abubakar: Kept his word by handing over to an elected government after a short tenure

Table 1: Summary of major constitutional developments in Nigeria from 1914 to date

S/No	Name of Constitution	Effective Year	Size of Central Legislature	Official Members	Unofficial or Appointed Members	Elected Members	Relationship B/W Central & Regional Legislatures	Key Features
1.	Lugard	1914	Nil	All	Nil	Nil	Legislative Council for Lagos only; Gov-Gen makes laws for rest of country.	- Totalitarian. - Subject only to Colonial Office, London
2	Clifford	1922	46	27	19	4 – Directly: Lagos - 3 Calabar - 1	- Legislative Council for Southern Nigeria only; North not represented	- Introduced elective principle for first time - Introduced principle of separate development by treating North & South differently.
3.	Richards	1946	44	16	28	4 - Directly 24 - Indirectly	- Central Council + 3 regional Councils + Regional House of Chiefs for North only	- Maintained separate development. - Introduced Regionalism – East, West, North - Most criticized and short-lived
4.	Macpherson	1951	**149** 136 Elected 13 Appointed	7	6 – Special Interest Groups	136	- Central Council + 3 regional Councils	- Maintained Regionalism - Introduced first Council of Ministers; Permitting local involvement in exec. govt. - Expanded overall political space for Nigerians – Executive, Legislative
5.	Lyttelton (Amendment)	1954	**184** + Speaker & 3 Ex-Officio members	1	3	184	- Central Council; 3 Regional Houses of Assembly. -Regional Assemblies now free of Central Assembly	- Expanded Council of Ministers to 13. - Created 2 Regional House of Chiefs for North & West only. None for East. - Colonial Govs. held veto power
6.	Independence (Robertson)	1960	**357** 45 – Senate 312 – House of Reps	Nil	Nil	All	- 2-chamber Central legislature + Regional legislatures	- Introduced bi-cameral Legislature for first time: Senate & H.O. Reps - Maintained British Parliamentary system (Majority party forms Govt.) - Queen of England is Head of State
7.	1st Republic	1963	Same	Nil	Nil	All	Same	- Proclaimed Nigeria a Republic and dropped Queen of England as Head of State - Queen Replaced by indigenous Governor-General
8.	2nd Republic	1979	**469** 109 – Senate 360 – House of Reps	Nil	Nil	All	2-chamber central legislature + State Assemblies	- Introduced American Presidential system (Head of Govt. elected directly by the people – not party) - Multi-party democracy
9.	3rd Republic	1993	469	Nil	Nil	All	Same	- Strictly 2 party democracy - Never fully operational
10	4th Republic	1999	469:	Nil	Nil	All	Same	- Return to multi-party democracy

Chapter 7: Development of Political Parties in Nigeria

Six key periods may be recognized in the history of modern political parties in Nigeria:

1. Pre-World War 2 Period (1914 – 1939)
2. Race to Independence Period (1944 – 1960)
3. Period of Internal Upheavals and Rise of Minority Parties (1960 – 1966)
4. First Attempt at Multi-Ethnic Parties (1978 – 1983)
5. Two-Party Ideology Period (1992

Pre-World War 2 Period (1914 – 1939)

This phase was made possible by the Clifford Constitution of 1922 which provided for elective positions in the parliamentary council for the first time. The two main political parties of this era were the Nigerian National Democratic Party (NNDP) founded by Herbert Macaulay in 1923, and the Nigerian Youth Movement (NYM) founded by Dr. Eyo Ita in 1933. During this period, politics was an elitist affair.

The activities of both political parties were limited to the coastal enclaves of Lagos and Calabar, although NYM was genuinely Nigerian in outlook and multi-ethnic in membership. For instance, at one time Dr. Kofo Abayomi was its president, Ernest Ikoli was vice president and H.O. Davies was secretary. Nnamdi Azikiwe, Obafemi Awolowo, Samuel Akintola and Adeyemo Alakija all joined later at one point or the other.

The manifestos of these early parties were also limited to demands for more representation, greater job opportunities and fairer treatment of locals.

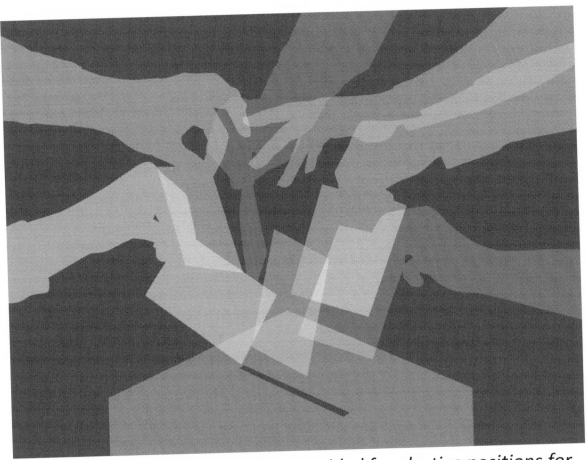

Figure 51: The 1922 Constitution provided for elective positions for the first time.

Race to Independence Period (1944 – 1960)

This phase derived its energy from events of the Second World War, particularly the breaking of the myth of European superiority. The leading parties of this period included the National Council of Nigeria and the Cameroons (NCNC, founded 1944), the Action Group (AG, founded 1951) and the Northern People's Congress (NPC, founded 1951). By this time, the NYM had broken up and its members dissolved into newer parties notably AG and NCNC. NCNC was later renamed National Convention of Nigerian Citizens.

The parties of this era were populist in orientation and, unlike their predecessors, derived their membership strength from the regional hinterlands and at times across several regions of the country. They were also bolder – not just asking for better treatment of locals but fearlessly demanding for self rule and an end to colonialism.

Although the NCNC started as a pan-Nigeria party, the AG and NPC were more regional in outlook, recruiting members chiefly from the West and North respectively. The name Northern People's Congress clearly indicates the orientation at that time. By the end of 1952 however, all the parties were effectively perceived as regional - with NCNC under Azikiwe now seen as a largely Eastern party, although party leaders insisted otherwise. These parties became the main instruments of nationalist agitation, eventually leading to independence in 1960.

Figure 52: The parties of this era fearlessly demanded for self rule and an end to colonialism

Period of Internal Upheavals and Rise of Minority Parties (1960 – 1966)

In this phase, the major national and regional parties began to splinter, unable to accommodate some of the many minority interests within them. Although this trend actually started from the 1950s, it peaked in the early 1960s, shortly after independence.

Some of the notable new parties of this period included the United Middle Belt Congress (UMBC, 1957), Nigerian National Democratic Party (NNDP, 1964), and United Progressive Grand Alliance (UPGA, 1964). Others were Bornu Youth Movement (BYM), Igala Union (IU), Igbira Tribal Union (ITU), Niger Delta Congress (NDC) and Midwest Democratic Front (MDF), etc. They stood for many ethnic, linguistic and other interest groups which felt dominated, marginalized or insufficiently represented in the bigger parties.

Whatever their size or inclination, all the parties went into dissolution in 1966 following Nigeria's first military coup which ousted the First Republic.

Figure 53: Splinter parties emerged as bigger ones were unable to accommodate minority interests

First Attempt at Multi-Ethnic Parties (1978 – 1983)

After 12 long years of forced vacation occasioned by crises, civil war and military rule, Nigeria's surviving political elite re-assembled in 1978 on the eve of the Second Republic. This time, obviously "wizened" by the First Republic experience, they all sought to be national in outlook and membership. Thus there was the National Party of Nigeria (NPN), the Unity Party of Nigeria (UPN), The Nigerian Peoples' Party (NPP) and the People's Redemption Party (PRP).

The names of these parties signified noble intentions, but the reality turned out differently. The presence and influence of First Republic political warhorses like Obafemi Awolowo, Nnamdi Azikiwe and Aminu Kano among them brought back old memories. Soon, these men emerged as their parties' presidential flag-bearers. Members of the public believed nothing had changed and that the country was back to its old ways of regional associations.

In retrospect, it might have been better if these men were persuaded to stay away. But they fought to enforce their constitutional rights to freedom of association. This phase lasted only about 5 years before the military struck again.

Figure 54: Parties of the Second Republic sought to be national in outlook and membership

Two-Party Ideology Period (1992 – 1993)

This was an experimental phase in Nigerian political history carried out by a military dictator, General Ibrahim Babangida. He reasoned that in most democratic countries of the world, politics ultimately revolved around two major parties – Right wing versus Left wing; Republicans versus Democrats; Conservatives versus Labor; Nationalists versus Socialists. The rest of the parties, he reasoned, were largely irrelevant, only representing different shades of the two primary colors.

Mindful of the bitter regional and ethnic rivalries that marked the country's earlier democratic experience, Babangida decided to forge Nigeria's political elite into either of the two ideological boxes - one "a little to the right" which he called the National Republican Convention (NRC); the other "a little to the let" which he called the Social Democratic Party (SDP).

Looking back, it appears the intention was good and the logic fairly well reasoned. Reluctantly, Nigerian politicians lined up behind their preferred parties. In the subsequent election, SDP's Moshood Abiola clearly beat NRC's Bashir Tofa to emerge President-in-waiting. Nigerians hailed this as a rare case of constitutional wizardry that could replace ethnic & regional politics with politics of ideology for good. But in an unprecedented move, Babangida suspended the results before the final tally and eventually "annulled" the polls.

Figure 55: Moshood Abiola of the SDP, winner of the 1993 two-party presidential election that was nullified.

Figure 56: Bashir Tofa: Contested and lost under the NRC

His reasons for this remain shrouded in mystery. Many believe the outcome did not go according to script. Whatever happened, that bold political experiment ended suddenly and disastrously. M. K. O. Abiola went into hiding and later emerged to claim his mandate. He was arrested and put in detention where he later died suddenly in July, 1998. Meanwhile, Nigeria slipped back into political limbo.

Between 1993 and 1998, a number of shadow political organizations were active in the country as "pro-democracy" or civil society organizations. These included National Democratic Coalition (NADECO) among others. They continued to put pressure on the military government to leave and open up the space once and for all for proper democratic institutions.

As soon as the relevant constitutional framework came into operation by 1998, many of those associations and organizations dissolved into formal political parties as discussed in the next phase.

Free Market Phase (1999 to date)

General Abdulsalami Abubakar (who took over following the sudden death of General Sanni Abacha in 1998) gets the credit for being the midwife of the current phase of political party history in Nigeria. A professional soldier with little or no ambition for politics, he set about returning the country to civilian democratic rule in the shortest possible time. Perhaps this explains the absence of deep ideological thinking behind the 1999 Constitution which forms the basis for the current political party arrangement. Perhaps it demonstrates the quality of keeping things simple or going back to basics.

Under this arrangement, practically every Nigerian is at liberty to register a party as long as basic minimum requirements are met. As a result, there are scores of parties in the books of the national electoral commission at any time, although only a handful are active or have won seats in parliament. These include the Peoples Democratic Party (PDP), All Progressive Congress (APC) which came from a merger of several parties, Labour Party (LP) and All Progressives Grand Alliance (APGA) among several others.

The only discernible idea behind this "free market" approach seems to be that eventually the strong will survive and the weak will die; and so there is no need to interfere with a natural process. Only time will tell how true this is, and how well this thinking will serve this politically embattled nation.

Figure 57

Summary & Conclusions

Like nearly every other modern nation, Nigeria was forged from the merger of several ethnic, cultural and linguistic groups – often for administrative or political reasons. Unlike many other nations however, there is very little evidence of genuine nation-building efforts in the years following its formation. Administrative and economic amalgamation was not followed by mental, cultural and political integration.

The British colonial authorities whose idea Nigeria was, were either unconcerned or actively sabotaging the emergence of a single, united national spirit, for fear of the people ganging up against them. This is neither strange nor unique; it is in the nature of colonial or foreign rule worldwide, down the ages, to play one group against the other.

What is perhaps strange is that educated Nigerians and politicians who subsequently took over from the British appeared solely interested in filling the new positions of power and status opened up by the British, especially following the 1951 Constitution. As young men and women with scant experience in public service and limited exposure to global geo-politics, they failed woefully to grasp the bigger picture, overcome individual greed and rise above colonial manipulation.

What happened between 1945 and 1960 was simply a scramble for and partition of Nigeria among various individuals and interest groups. Ethnic rivalry, dressed as regionalism, was a cloak which masked raw individualism and avarice. Later, it assumed a life of its own. Little wonder that newly independent Nigeria quickly descended into anarchy as soon as the British let. General J.T.U. Aguiyi-Ironsi's attempt at unitary government was poorly considered, ill-timed and dead on arrival. In failing to put on trial and punish Nigeria's first coup plotters, he failed to arrest inter-ethnic suspicion and left the door open for further crisis. General Yakubu Gowon's creation of 12 states, though a political masterstroke, appeared to have come too late to halt the drift. Besides, it was not a genuine act of nation-building but one solely designed to weaken the opponent – not settle a widening national rift.

The civil war was a logical and tragic consequence of consistently poor choices and actions on all sides. No one plants weeds and gathers wheat. Looking back, even the lofty declaration of "No Victor, No Vanquished" by the victorious federal side at the end of hostilities appears to have been more sloganeering than social engineering.

Nearly half a century after the civil war ended, Nigerians are not happier about the state of their union than they were on the eve of war. Although they get on quite well with one another on inter-personal, social and even commercial levels, inter-group distrust and bitter rivalry persist especially on the political front.

Widespread agitations for true federalism, resource control, restructuring and even secession are clear signals that cultural, social, political and human amalgamation has not progressed on the right course since 1914.

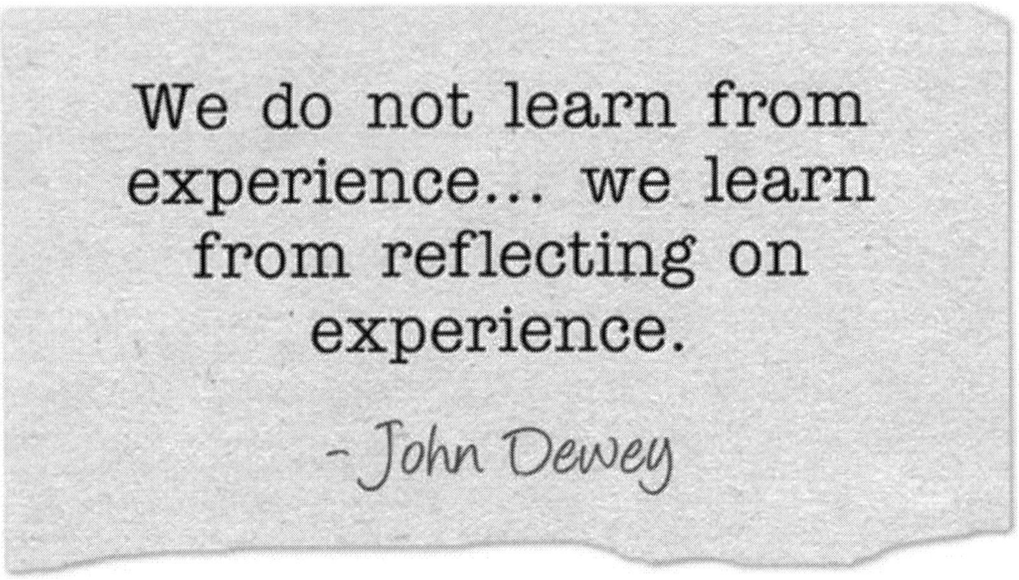

> We do not learn from experience... we learn from reflecting on experience.
>
> — John Dewey

Figure 58

FURTHER READING

Chapter 1

History of Sokoto City and Sokoto Caliphate, Naijasky.com

Sokoto Caliphate, Wikipedia

Sokoto Caliphate in the Nineteenth Century, worldhistory.biz

Oyo Empire, Britannica.com

Oyo Empire, Wikipedia

Oyo Empire, Logbaby.com

Adiele Afigbo, *Igbo History & Society: The Essays of Adiele Afigbo, Africa* Word Press, 2005

Victor Uchendu, *The Igbo in Southeast Nigeria (Case Studies in Cultural Anthropology)*, Reinhold, 1965

Elizabeth Isichei, *A History of African Societies to 1870*, Cambridge University Press, 1997

Ukpuru.tumblr.com

Chapter 2

H. L. Peacock, "Europe and the Third World 1953 – 1978," in *A History of Modern Europe 1789 – 1978,* Heineman, 1980

Frederick Lugard, *The Dual Mandate in British Tropical Africa*, Blackwood & Sons, 1922

Charles Miller, "An Entertainment in Imperialism," **The Lunatic Express**, 1971

I. F. Nicholson, *The Administration of Nigeria 1900 to 1960*, Oxford University Press, 1969

R. Martin, *History of the British Colonies*, London, 1835

Leonard Woolf, *Empire and Commerce in Africa*, London, 1920

W. Geary, *Nigeria under British Rule*, London, 1927

K.O. Dike, *Trade and Politics in the Niger Delta 1830 – 1895*, Oxford, 1956

Chapter 3

James Coleman, *Nigeria: Background to Nationalism*, California, 1971

Tekena Tamuno, *Herbert Macaulay; Nigerian Patriot*, Heineman, 1976

Nnamdi Azikiwe, *Renascent Africa*, Routledge, 1968

Toyin Falola & Saheed Aderinto, *Nigeria, Nationalism and Writing History*, Rochester, 2010

Chapter 4

Oluwole Odumosu, *The Nigerian Constitution: history and development*, Sweet & Maxwell, London, 1963

B.O. Nwabueze, *A Constitutional History of Nigeria*, Hurst, London, 1982

S. G. Ehindero, *The Constitutional Development of Nigeria 1849 – 1989*, Ehindero, Lagos, 1991

Chapter 5

Anthony Akinola, *Democracy in Nigeria; Thoughts and Selected Commentaries*, Rossendale, 2013

J. O. Ojiako, *Nigeria: Yesterday, Today and...?*, Africana, 1981

"Verdict" (editorial), **West Africa Magazine**, June 16, 1962

Bola Ige, *People, Politics And Politicians of Nigeria 1940-1979*, Heinemann, 1995

Remi Oyeyemi, *Samuel Ladoke Akintola and History*, nigeriaworld.com 23/06/2003

Adewale Ademoyega, *Why we struck: The Story of the First Nigerian Coup*, Evans, 1981

Ben Gbulie, *Nigeria's Five Majors: Coup d'état of 15th January 1966, first inside account*, Africana, 1981

Chapter 6

Peter Baxter, Biafra: *The Nigerian Civil War 1967 – 1970*, Helion, 2014

Ayuba Mshelia, Araba: *Let's Separate —The Story of the Nigerian Civil War*, AuthorHouse, 2012

Chinua Achebe, *There was a Country,* Penguin, 2012

Chapter 7

Anthony Akinola, *Party Coalitions in Nigeria; History, Trends and Prospects*, Safari, 2014

54098615R00076

Made in the USA
San Bernardino, CA
18 September 2019